M. + J. Walzer
April 1984
Princeton

BIBLICAL PROSE PRAYER

THE TAUBMAN LECTURES IN JEWISH STUDIES:
SIXTH SERIES

BIBLICAL PROSE PRAYER

*As a Window to the Popular Religion of
Ancient Israel*

MOSHE GREENBERG

UNIVERSITY OF CALIFORNIA PRESS
Berkeley   Los Angeles   London

University of California Press
Berkeley and Los Angeles, California

University of California Press, Ltd.
London, England

Library of Congress Cataloging in Publication Data

Greenberg, Moshe.
  Biblical prose prayer.

  (The Taubman lectures in Jewish studies. Sixth series)
  Includes bibliographical references and index.
  1. Prayer—Biblical teaching.   2. Bible. O.T.—
Prayers—History and criticism.   3. Bible.   O.T.—Criti-
cism, interpretation, etc.   I. Title.   II. Series.
BS1199.P68G73   1983   248.3   83-47662
ISBN 0-520-05011-8
ISBN 0-520-05012-6 (pbk.)

Printed in the United States of America

1 2 3 4 5 6 7 8 9

CONTENTS

THE TAUBMAN PROFESSORSHIP AND LECTURES

The Herman P. and Sophia Taubman Visiting Professorship in Jewish Studies was established at the University of California, Berkeley in 1975 by grants from Milton I. Taubman and the Taubman Foundation; an equal sum was contributed by the family of Maurice Amado, Walter A. Haas, Daniel E. Koshland, Madeline Haas Russell, and Benjamin H. Swig. Distinguished scholars in the fields of Jewish studies are invited to teach at Berkeley for the enrichment of students, and to give open lectures for the benefit of the public at large. Publication of the lectures is made possible by a special gift of the Taubman Foundation.

ACKNOWLEDGMENTS

Years of studying nonpsalmic prayer in the Hebrew Scriptures culminated in an article I prepared on the subject, in 1980, for the last volume of the Hebrew *Encyclopaedia Biblica.* After completing the article I realized how meager its conceptual framework was, and attempted to elaborate on it in class lectures in the Hebrew University during 1980-1981. It was then that I was honored by an invitation to serve at the University of California, Berkeley, as the visiting Taubman professor of Jewish studies during the fall and winter of 1981-1982—an office to which the duty of delivering a series of public lectures is attached. This afforded me a welcome opportunity to consolidate my still somewhat amorphous thoughts, and seek the implications of the fact that the Scriptures represent lay prayers as extemporized—a fact that has not excited much scholarly attention.

I hope that some reflection of the exhilaration I felt in composing these lectures will be apparent to one who reads them in their present form—only slightly revised from the form in which they were delivered. I would have the reader take that as a tribute to the benign and facilitating academic environment at Berkeley, enhanced, for me, by the hospitality extended to me and my wife by colleagues and friends, old and new. In connection with these lectures, my thanks go to the following, who discussed aspects of the lectures with me, and whose comments left a mark on them: Richard Webster, Hannah Bloch, Meir Sternberg, Jacob Milgrom and Robert Alter.

LECTURE 1

Why are we moderns still drawn to the ancient Hebrew Scriptures? For one thing, since we are (at least descended from) Jews and Christians, we recognize in the Scriptures, whether we are religious or not, a spiritual and cultural patrimony: they are a source, containing paradigms of some of our distinctive and cherished values. A child is fascinated by the lineaments and the character of his ancestors, in which he seeks and finds the antecedents of his own identity. In like manner we peruse the Scriptures, which delineate our ancestors—literally, as the Jews hold, or by divine engrafting, as do the Christians—for the sources of our own identity and the values that link us to our nearest forebears. Finding them there, we have the assurance that we are not spiritual foundlings, but heirs of a rich and marvelously diverse tradition sprung from their roots.

Another reason for the Scriptures' lasting appeal is the surprising frequency with which, even without a preacher's embellishment, they seem to touch on our concerns. Our times differ radically from those of the Bible, and both our knowledge and our ignorance, our perplexities and our hopes, are beyond its scope. Yet, strange to say, we are still able to be stirred by the biblical representation of the main issues of human existence. Hebrew Scriptures offer a panorama of individual and collective lives and a variety of reflections and observations on them that constantly involve elemental values. Motives of behavior are stated and judged, or beg to be supplied by the reader. Causes are assigned to events, usually in the divine order; but when events are opaque, the observer's perplexity is candidly expressed and the failure of conventional explanation starkly exposed. The reader of the Scriptures soon finds himself diverted from ephemeral concerns to a consideration of fundamental, lasting issues, and these are dealt with in a plain and simple way that somehow bypasses our subtleties, complexities, and sophistication. By reducing issues to essentials, and thus making it impossible for the reader to escape them, the Scriptures work an effect like that of a child's blunt question or uninhibited comment on grown-up conduct. As a child's remark is capable of exposing a disturbing truth hidden under rationalization and self-deception, so the ancient writings invite us constantly to consider that beneath the glorious achievements of civilization stands the human being, a frail needy creature whose happiness still depends on discovering what it is, and why—without having had any say in the matter—it has been called into being.

Religion answers such existential questions by reference to a transcendent realm. The visible, tangible, phenomenal world does not in itself satisfy the restless soul's quest for meaning; the meaning of the mundane derives from its relation to the supermundane.[1] Biblical religion, and its offspring—Judaism, Christianity, and Islam—conceptualize the essence of the transcendent realm as one God, the source and ground of all being and all meaning. Single and all embracing, the concept of God integrates the cosmos, lending it coherence, consistency and thus intelligibility.

For his well-being, man must communicate with the transcendent realm, in order both to receive such knowledge and information as will enable him to conform to its nature and its will (if it is anthropomorphized, as it is in biblical religion), and to be able to have recourse to it in time of need. With the biblical God is "the fountain of life" (Ps. 36:10), he is himself depicted as "the fountain of living water" (Jer. 2:13); hence connection with him is a link to the vital source of all blessing: one who visits the temple "carries away blessing from YHWH" (Ps. 24:5). Central to religion, therefore, are institutions of two-way communication with the transcendent; in the Bible, oracles are given to man in three authorized ways—dreams, the priestly oracle and prophets (1 Sam. 28:6)—and man resorts to God through worship and prayer. There seems, however, to be a difference between the ways of God and those of man. God's dream-revelations to Israelites are plain, and their sense is immediately given; conformably, we hear of no professional dream-interpretation in biblical Israel. (I leave aside here the dreams of Pharaoh and Nebuchadnezzar; their riddle-character recalls the connotation of mystery and equivocation that attaches to the terms "oracle" and "oracular," corresponding to the pagan conception of the relation of the supermundane realm to mankind, which is far from consistently or uniformly friendly. Note, however, that Joseph and Daniel are able to interpret the riddle-dreams, not through expertise, but through a special gift of God.) The technique of the priestly lot in Israel was also simple: questions to be answered "yes" or "no" were put to it, and its unequivocal response needed no expert to decipher it. Israel's prophets too were not schooled and

learned professionals, but men called from all walks of
life by the free choice of God; nor was their message so
cryptic that it had to be interpreted to the public. In
sum: the ways in which God communicated with men
were all simple and minimally mediated; no human
expertise was needed to make his message understand-
able.[2] Such uncomplicated access to God's word—compared with the dependence on legions of experts in
paganism—accords with the good will toward man that
motivates the biblical God: it is for him to give and for
man to receive in humble obedience and loyalty.

The ways of human communication with God appear
more contingent upon mediation and prescription; indeed the most prominent forms of worship and prayer
in the Bible seem to leave little room for free, simple,
spontaneous expression.

The institution of the sanctuary and its rites and celebrations is by divine decree, involving the finest details
of architecture and ritual. The central act of worship at
the sanctuary, sacrifice, is in the hands of God's elected
priesthood and their consecrated auxiliaries. Apart from
the confession of one who offered a reparation-sacrifice,
the laity had no role in this worship. Moreover, if we
can rely on the biblical data, not even the priests had
anything to say by way of prayer accompanying the
sacrifices; besides the priests' confession on the Day of
Atonement, no verbal expression of homage or petition
is so much as hinted at in all the extensive detail of sacri-
ficial prescriptions. Clearly this was not an area in
which any human sentiment of devotion could find a
voice. To be sure, there was a verbal component of
sanctuary worship—the song that was part of temple
celebrations, at least on festive days, according to

meager evidence garnered mainly from the psalms. Amos refers to it when, speaking for God, he denounces Israel's sacrifices: "Take away from me the noise of your songs; to the melody of your lyres I will not listen" (5:23). As Isaiah depicts Israel's participation in the future triumph of God, he says: "But for you there will be a song as in the night when a sacred festival is held" (30:29). Among those who returned from the Babylonian exile to Jerusalem were "the temple singers, of the descendants of Asaph" (Ezra 2:41); since such a class could not have sprung up in the sanctuary-less exile, its existence must go back at least to the latter days of Judah's monarchy.

Was the institution of temple singers, which is not provided for in the laws, conceived to be a human initiative, and their song a human invention? The vehement censure of Jeroboam's innovations in worship throughout the book of Kings shows how blameworthy human meddling in divine institutions was held to be. Not surprisingly, therefore, the Chronicler bestows divine legitimation on temple-song, an office that was venerable by his time: the temple singers were ordained by God through the agencies of David, the man of God, as well as the seer Gad and the prophet Nathan (2 Chron. 8:14; 29:25). Furthermore, their song was inspired: "David . . . set apart for the service certain of the sons of Asaph, Heman, and Jeduthun, who should prophesy with lyres, harps, and cymbals" (1 Chron. 25:1; the verb prophesy is repeated twice more in the following two verses). Now several canonical psalms are ascribed to these singers (Asaph, Pss. 73-83; Heman, Ps. 88; Jeduthun, Ps. 39); these, like all the psalms in the psalter have a distinctive style, phraseology, and vocabulary that are the mark of a school of liturgical poets. It has long been noted that, despite the genuine fervor that pervades the psalms, for the most part, the circumstances they describe lack particularity; they speak in general terms of individual and communal distress and salvation, of God's mercies and wonders in history and nature. Whatever their origin, it seems that they functioned as stock compositions of trained liturgical poets, utilized by individuals and assemblies at temple celebrations; so whether we follow the late biblical concept of the Chronicler, that the temple-song was inspired "prophesying," or the scholarly judgment that it was a product of schooled guildsmen, it was not a realm of immediate, free invention.

One speaks tentatively of these matters because the psalmody of the Bible lacks an attested life setting. Life settings have been conjectured on the basis of allusions in the psalms, but they carry no real conviction. All that can be said with any firmness is that their peculiar style and language confirm the traditional ascriptions to David, Asaph, etc., in the sense that these men were regarded as professional poets; this explains the eloquence of the psalms and the noble religious sentiments that are frequent in them. Though the laity may have appropriated them for their use at the temple—Hannah's psalm (1 Sam. 2:1-10) is a fine example of this—we cannot draw from psalms or their conjectured life settings a picture of everyday, spontaneous piety in biblical Israel.

The two most prominent and ample sources of information about the religious practice of ancient Israel— the temple rituals and the psalms—are thus deficient as mirrors of the commoners' religion; both are prescriptions of the schooled; they belong to a class of experts.

The piety of the populace was mediated and probably refined through them. But for a clue to unmediated, direct forms of popular piety we must turn elsewhere—to the prayers embedded in the narratives of Scripture.

As used here, prayer refers to nonpsalmic speech to God—less often about God—expressing dependence, subjection, or obligation; it includes petition, confession, benediction, and curse (but excludes references to nothing more than oracle-seeking). The term narrative is used loosely to include not only story but also prophetic oracle (e.g., the prayers of Jeremiah)—again, any nonpsalmic context. What distinguishes all these prayers is that they appear to be freely composed in accordance with particular life-settings; their putative authors and their function are supplied by their context.

Here are some statistics on biblical prayers, and their relation to other forms of worship. References to the actual occurrence of temple rites—as distinct from legislation on them—appear about ninety times in Hebrew Scriptures; praying and prayers are mentioned, outside of Psalms, about 140 times. In well over half the cases, it is the act of prayer alone that is mentioned, for example: "The Israelites were terribly afraid [of the Egyptians], and cried to YHWH" (Exod. 14:10). In the rest, the verbal formulation of the prayer is given—some ninety-seven prayer texts. In quantity, their number is just under two-thirds of the number of psalms—150. Thirty-eight of the formulated prayers are spoken by lay people; fifty-nine by such leading men as kings or prophets. They are distributed throughout the historical books, from Genesis to Chronicles; among the prophets, Jeremiah stands out for his prayers. Yet, in spite of this considerable quantity of evidence, the study of it, and its utilization in the description of biblical religion has hitherto been negligible.[3] How is that to be explained?

I venture to suggest that precisely its embedded quality has caused scholars to overlook its possible significance apart from its story context. This material is not an immediate witness to the prayers of ancient Israel. Every prayer text is part of a literary artifact. Even the mere report of an act of prayer represents a deliberate choice of the narrator, let alone the verbal formulation of a prayer embedded in a story. Samson (granting he existed) cannot be supposed to have prayed only twice in his lifetime, though only two prayers are recorded in his story. Nor can we think that by including only two prayers the narrator would have us believe anything of the kind. We must surely suppose, rather, that their inclusion just there and in that wording served the narrator's purpose. Hence, it cannot be excluded—it is, on the contrary, likely—that the wording of Samson's prayers is as much an artifice as the rest of the narrative. This doubt that the embedded prayers are veridical— that the literary record corresponds to what, in fact, the characters prayed—is, I conjecture, the ground for the scholarly neglect of them. If so, it is a wrongheaded ground, for even if it is granted that the prayers are not veridical, that does not foreclose their being verisimilar. In this matter, as in other aspects of the Scriptural message, verisimilitude may be as valuable as veridicality. (Recall Aristotle's dictum [*Poetics*, 9] that poetry—that is, artistic creation—is "something more philosophic and of graver import than history.") To determine their verisimilitude we must ask: are the circumstances and formulations of prayer in the Scriptures such as raise doubts as to whether they might have been so prayed in ancient Israel? Are the various literary prayers so conditioned by their narrative contexts as to be formally distinct, so that we must regard the art of the given narrator as decisive in their formulation? Can we find analogies in social speech for the forms of prayer, so that the notion that the narrators loosely and freely invented the prayers they put in the mouths of characters seems unlikely? If the answers to these questions support the view that the forms of Scriptural prayer represent the forms actually in use in ancient Israel, we shall have made an advance in our knowledge of ancient popular religion. If, along the way, we learn something about the way in which the prayer texts serve the narratives, we shall have gained a bit of insight into an aspect of the literary art of the Bible. The prospect of such gains arouses our interest in pursuing the inquiry.

Petitionary prayer, including intercession (i.e., a petition one person makes on behalf of and for the good of another), is the most frequently attested type, and affords the greatest number of formulated examples. We begin, therefore, by passing in review some of these, going from the simple to the complex.

Numbers 12:13. After Aaron and Miriam defamed Moses, God rebuked them and inflicted leprosy on Miriam. Aaron pleaded with Moses on her behalf, whereupon Moses cried to YHWH:

> *address:* O God, pray!—
> *petition:* Pray heal her!

Judges 16:28. Samson entreated God thus before pulling down the Philistine temple on himself and his triumphant captors:

> *address:* O Lord YHWH
> *petition:* Pray remember me and pray strengthen me only this
> time, O God,
> *motivation:* that I may exact retribution for one of my two eyes
> from the Philistines!

Genesis 32:10-13. Fearing his approaching brother Esau, Jacob divided his people and property into two companies, in the hope that at least one would escape an attack by Esau; then he prayed:

> *address:* God of my father Abraham,
> and God of my father Isaac,
> YHWH,
> *(description:)* who said to me, 'Return to your land and kin and
> I will make you prosperous,'
> *self-deprecation:* I do not deserve all the acts of constant care
> and all the fidelity that you have shown your servant;
> *(detail:)* for with nothing but my staff I crossed the Jordan here,
> but now I have become two companies.
> *petition:* Save me from the hand of my brother, from the hand
> of Esau,
> *description of distress:* for I fear that he may come and kill me,
> mothers and children alike.
> *motivation:* But you said, 'I will surely make you prosperous,
> and I will make your offspring like the sands of the sea
> that are too numerous to be counted.'

These three petitionary prayers allow the following generalizations. Such prayer arises out of a particular, momentary need, and may be uttered anywhere—even in a pagan temple. Unmediated, it opens with an address, invoking God by name (YHWH or a surrogate), to which may be added descriptive attributes. The heart of the prayer, the petition, is formulated in "imperatives"—here, of course, expressing what the pray-er begs God to do, rather than commands him. In the last two examples, the petition is followed by a ground, or a motive-sentence—offering what is hoped will be a persuasive reason for God to comply. In the third, most complex prayer, the petition is preceded by self-deprecation, which serves, in part to allay resentment at what may seem to be lack of appreciation of all God had done for Jacob; this component may be called the facilitation of the petition.

The pattern of address, petition, and motivation, in longer prayers with various additions (e.g., description of distress), repetitions or lengthening of given parts (e.g., by adding epithets and attributes to the address), appears, not at all, but in most petitionary prayers. It is a natural pattern, deriving logically from the circumstances of the prayer. The pray-er needs a good that only God can bestow. He appeals to God on the basis of an established relation with him, which he invokes in several ways: by aptly chosen epithets and descriptive attributes, and especially in the motivating sentence. In the motivation, the pray-er appeals to a common value, some identity of interest between him and God, some ground on which he can expect God's sympathy and a demonstration of solidarity. Thus all the elements surrounding the petition, before it and after it, aim at establishing a bond between the pray-er and God, an identity of interest—a primary aim of prayer rhetoric.[4]

The opening invocation of God by name—usually his proper name YHWH—establishes contact with an invisible presence.[5] A surrogate may be used, if the occasion calls for it: in Moses's laconic prayer, consisting of four monosyllables, a monosyllabic surrogate, 'el, "God," serves for an invocation. Epithets and descriptive phrases may be added, and these invite reflection on their significance (even though a suitable significance cannot always be found out [the same must be said for some of the surrogates]). Samson's "O Lord (YHWH)" —a common courtly epithet—gains its peculiar force from comparison with the blunt familiarity of the opening of his earlier prayer, "You granted this great victory through the agency of your servant" (Judg. 15:18). Just that consciousness of being near God that is expressed in the content of that line allowed omission of an invocation; on the contrary, Samson's sense of having been abandoned by God during years of degrading captivity underlies the diffidence suggested by the courtly invocation of his final prayer. (The suggestion is borne out by the substance of the petition, "Pray remember me. . . .") In Jacob's prayer, the epithets "God of my father Abraham, God of my father Isaac," run ahead of the proper name, YHWH, to prepare the way for its reception. Jacob related himself to God not directly, but as the child of God's favorites, first of all his grandfather, then his father. Thus from the outset he intimates his own unworthiness, which he proceeds to enlarge on explicitly in the self-deprecating sequel. The epithets in both prayers affirm a relation of the pray-er to God, which creates at least the color of a divine obligation toward him. If YHWH is Samson's Lord, then Samson is his servant; by acknowledging this relation, Samson intends to move God to act on a lord's duty to protect his clients. Jacob chooses epithets implying that a son of favorites ought to be given a hearing even if, of himself, he has little to commend him. Both choices of epithets show the concern of pray-ers to affirm a relation to God as the basis of their call on his attention.

The motivating sentence of a petitionary prayer is revealing for the pray-er's conception of God, since one is persuaded to do what is shown to be most consonant with one's attributes and one's interests. For Samson, to empower him to exact retribution (*nqm*) for the mutilation and humiliation inflicted on him was motive enough for God to comply with his prayer. Rough and self-centered, this motive accords with the character Samson displays throughout his adventures. But it is also no departure from an attribute of the biblical God. Derivatives of *nqm* denote the exaction of retribution in an extraordinary, extralegal, extra-procedural manner ("retribution" in this context means "dealing back to one what he has dealt out"; see the setting of Judg. 15:7, namely, vv. 3-11). The Israelite is expressly forbidden to exact *nqm* from his fellow (Lev. 19:18), and it is the sign of a saintly, noble person that he commits his *nqm* to God (David, 1 Sam. 24:12; Jeremiah, Jer. 15:15, etc.). For YHWH is properly God of *nqm* (e.g., Nah. 1:2; Ps. 94:1); to him belongs the ultimate redressing of all wrongs, and by whatever means he wills. Of the forty-four nominal forms of *nqm*, thirty-five refer to acts of God; half the verbal forms have him as subject. But he may commit his *nqm* into human hands, in which case his cause and that of those humans are identified (e.g., Num. 31:2, 3). More especially, mortals doing God's work may exact *nqm* on their own (Josh. 10:13; 1 Sam. 14:24, 18:25). Here Samson, beyond all hope of ever seeing procedural justice done him for his injuries, entreats God to empower him to exact extraordinary retribution for himself—for him, there can be no other kind; and the God of *nqm* complies.[6]

The motivating sentence in Jacob's petition invokes God's earlier promise to make him prosperous and give him numerous offspring. This is at bottom an appeal to God's constancy, reliability, and trustworthiness—in Hebrew, his *ḥesed we'emet*. The ground for it has been well prepared in the foregoing lines. To the address, Jacob adds the description, "He who said to me, 'Return to your land and your kin and I will make you prosperous.'" In the course of deprecating himself, Jacob cites God's "acts of constancy and fidelity," namely, the providence that increased the size of his family till now it had become "two companies" (we cannot help admiring the adroitness with which Jacob turns his desperate stratagem to rhetorical advantage). In particularizing his distress, adjunct to his petition, he cites his fear of being annihilated, "mother with children." When, in the final, motivating sentence he combines God's promise of making him prosper with the promise of numerous progeny, he thus recapitulates items that have occurred all through the prayer. As the family God, as the author of a promise to deal well with Jacob which, trustworthy as he is, he has already honored, YHWH must be moved by the imminent peril to Jacob and his family—which is ultimately a threat to God's declared plan. Surely God will be true to his promise and defend his reputation for fidelity. Jacob's prayer is a model of rhetoric—a principle of which is to persuade the one appealed to that his interests and one's own coincide.

The fuller pattern of the prayers of Samson and Jacob contrast with Moses' five-word petition. Its brevity is highlighted by the immediately preceding appeal of Aaron, four times as long, that Moses forgive his offending siblings. The five words comprise the barest bones of a petitionary prayer, an address, and a petition. In so short a prayer, the repetition of the particle of plea, *na* ("pray"), stands out as imparting a special urgency to the request to heal Miriam of her horrible affliction. What does the brevity suggest? To the medievals, solicitude: "So that the Israelites might not say, 'His sister is in distress and he stands long in prayer'" (Rashi; to this some printings add, "Another interpretation: So that it might not be said, 'For his sister he prays long, for us he doesn't'"). However, if we compare the cases of Hannah and David, about each of whom it is expressly noted that their deep distress moved them to pray long (1 Sam. 1:12; 2 Sam. 12:16 ff.), we may be inclined to the contrary notion that such extreme brevity indicates Moses's distaste for the whole affair. He does not support his entreaty with a motive but banks on his favor with God to give it weight. That these five words represent an unenthusiastic, minimal compliance with Aaron's plea on Miriam's behalf is further suggested by the oblique pronominal reference to "her"; indeed throughout verses 11 to 14, neither Aaron nor Moses nor God refer to the disgraced woman by name.

Telling evidence of the Scriptural assumption of the universal capacity for prayer and its unlimited efficacy is found in the book of Jonah. The ship carrying Jonah away from his mission is beset by a storm; the refractory prophet confesses to the disconcerted sailors that he is its cause, since he is fleeing from his God's commandment. He recommends that they throw him into the sea, to which they respond by trying to row the boat to shore, for they are unwilling to incur the guilt of homicide. However, the storm's increasing vehemence frustrates them, so they prepare to throw Jonah overboard, in accord with his offer. Before acting they pray (Jon. 1:14):

> *address:* Please, YHWH!
> *petition:* Pray let us not perish on account of the life of this
>   man, and do not lay upon us the death of an innocent,
> *motivation:* For you, YHWH, have done as you pleased.

The heathen sailors, momentarily converted to ac-
knowledge Israel's God, pray in the familiar pattern of
address, petition, motivation.[7] Their prayer climaxes
their service to the story as a spiritually sensitive foil to
the unresponsive, finally lethargic, prophet. While he
slept in the teeth of the storm, they prayed each to his
God; while he refused to warn Nineveh away from dis-
aster, these heathen sailors risked their lives to save his;
whereas he was in rebellion against his God, they
acknowledged his sovereignty in their prayer to him. Inasmuch as they have just come to recognize YHWH,
their address to him contains no epithets. By repetition,
they express in their petition their anxiety over incurring
guilt for an action imposed on them by *force majeure*—
as they put it in the motivating sentence. The motive is
essentially an appeal to God's fairness: since Jonah has
confessed that the storm is caused by YHWH's displea-
sure with him, and since the storm's intensity only increased when they tried to save Jonah by putting him
ashore, thus thwarting them, YHWH has clearly sig-
nalled his wish to have Jonah thrown overboard. All
that the sailors know of this God is that there is no
avoiding his determination to get at Jonah, for he can
manipulate the elements at will. Acknowledging his
sovereignty in the motivating sentence, they exonerate
themselves by ascribing their action to it. Since what
they are about to do accords with the clear indication of
his will, in all fairness, he cannot hold them guilty for it.
Fairness (here, ultimately, consistency) is an attribute

that, in the biblical view, even the heathens recognize as divine, as in God's interest to confirm.

We may summarize our findings on petitionary prayer as follows:

The narratives depict such prayers as unconditioned by specific times, places and persons. Whenever one is in distress he may pray—even if he is in a pagan temple, and even if he is a pagan. Although the pray-er's status with God counts—for Aaron, in disgrace, appeals to God's favorite, Moses, to pray for Miriam (herself out of grace too)—and although the temple is the favored place of prayer (see, e.g., 1 Kings 8:28 ff.), it is not necessary to have a personal or local mediator; the cry of the distressed reaches God unaided.

Every human being is capable of formulating a petitionary prayer according to his need, not only such heroes as Moses and Jacob, but even such roughnecks as Samson, and even pagans.

The formulated prayers follow a simple pattern, consisting basically of address, petition, and motivating sentence, with freedom to add and subtract elements. The content of the prayers is tailored to the circumstances in which it arises; hence the prayers cannot be reused.

These features distinguish the embedded petitionary prayers from institutionalized forms of worship—sacrifice and other temple rituals and psalms. These are the properties of experts; their details are fixed and prescribed. A unit of them—a given sacrifice, a given psalm —is infinitely reusable or repeatable, since it is not determined by specific circumstances.

Finally, we have noted that the specificity of the embedded prayers means that they play a part in the argument of a narrative and its depiction of character: Moses's distaste (?), Samson's self-centered roughness, Jacob's smoothness, the heathen sailors' uprightness and piety.

The consistency of the pattern of petition, though drawn from samples in various sources—the Torah, the books of Judges, Jonah—raises the question of its origin. Is it a literary convention, shared by the various biblical authors, or does it reflect (in a literary mirror, to be sure) the actual practice of the times? Before we give our answer, we must consider the relation of prayer forms to analogous speech patterns used by the Israelites when speaking to each other.

LECTURE 2

The experience of God described in the Hebrew Scriptures is a kind of address by a personal being to the individual or the community. Events are perceived not merely as willed by God, but as signals conveying a divine message. When the sons of Jacob are entrapped by Joseph's concealed-cup trick, Judah apprehends their plight as divine retribution; "God," he says, "has discovered the crime of your servants" (Gen. 44:16). The main task of the classical prophets was to disclose to the people the divine messages hidden in (usually calamitous) events. Thus Amos interprets a series of natural and military disasters (Amos 4:6-11):

> It was I that gave you cleanness of teeth in all your cities,
> And lack of bread in all your places,
> But you did not return to me, declares YHWH.
> It was I that withheld the rain from you three months before harvest;
> And I sent rain on one city, but on another I did not send rain . . .
> So that two, three cities went begging to another city for water to drink yet were not satisfied,
> But you did not return to me, declares YHWH.
> I inflicted blight and mildew on you;
> The increase of your gardens, vineyards, figtrees and olive trees —locusts devoured,
> But you did not return to me, declares YHWH.
> I let plague loose among you, after the manner of Egypt;
> I slew your youths with the sword and caused your horses to be captured;
> I made the stench of your armies enter your nostrils;

> But you did not return to me, declares YHWH.
> I overturned you as Sodom and Gomorrah were supernaturally
>   overturned,
> And you were like a brand snatched from the burning,
> But you did not return to me, declares YHWH.

Events, then, are a sign language that God uses with men to communicate his favor and disfavor. But he also addresses man verbally, both directly and by mediaries, angelic and human. Such addresses reveal God as sentient, willing, purposeful—as having the attributes of a person; to express communication with such a being, biblical man employs the language of interhuman intercourse, since that is the only model available for interpersonal communication. Receiving God's address, man is "you" to God's "I"; addressing God, man is "I" to God's "you."

Speaking in the second person is only the most elemental form of biblical man's speech to God. When he prays, he uses words in patterns, and these patterns follow the analogy of interhuman speech patterns in comparable situations. The interhuman situation of petition may be analyzed as comprising the following elements: a need or distress; an unequal division of goods between petitioner and petitioned, leading the former to resort to the latter; affirmation of the given relationship between the two: the petitioner does not intend to destroy the relationship (he does not come with a club to take the goods by force), but to maintain himself on its basis; reliance on some common interest, some ground for solidarity between the two (else why should the petitioned be moved at all to part with his goods, or even to share them, for the benefit of the petitioner?).[1]

The closest human analogy to petitionary prayer will

be a petitionary address to a king or some other power-ful person. Here are a few phrases and terms that the two have in common. In the course of his intercession on behalf of Sodom and Gomorrah, Abraham mollifies God with the statement: "Let my Lord not be angry and I will speak" (Gen. 18:30), just as Judah opens his plea to Joseph with: "Please my lord, let your servant speak a word in my lord's hearing, and do not be angry with your servant" (Gen. 44:18), and Abigail's opens hers to David with: "Let the guilt, my lord, be mine! Let your maid speak in your hearing, and hear the word of your maid" (1 Sam. 25:24). In his apology, Meribaal (Mephi-bosheth) son of Saul throws himself on David's mercy with, "Do what is good in your eyes" (2 Sam. 19:28); the same phrase serves in a petitionary prayer of the community: "Do to us whatever is good in your eyes" (Judg. 10:15). The verb ṣaʿaq, "to shout," often used to denote prayer, also signifies suing for justice, as: "She went forth to 'shout' to the king about her house and her field" (2 Kings 8:3).

The affinity between suit and petitionary prayer is worth pausing over. Rachel named her maid's son Dan, "[God] has judged," explaining: "God has passed judg-ment on me and indeed has heard my prayer" (Gen. 30:6); thus she perceived her maid's childbearing as a verdict in her favor by God, in her suit against Leah (compare her explanation of the name she gave to her maid's next child, Naphtali: "I fought a titanic struggle with my sister, and I prevailed" [v. 8]). Such a concep-tion of petitionary prayer seems to underlie the common Hebrew noun $t^e pilla$, "prayer," and its cognate verb, $hitpallel$, "to pray." The basic sense of "estimate, judge, render a verdict" attaches to the verb $pillel$ (as in Jacob's prologue to blessing Joseph's sons: "I never reckoned [*lo pillalti*] on seeing your face" [Gen. 48:11]), and just once to the noun *tᵉpilla*, in Psalm 109:7—if parallelism is a trusty guide:

> *bᵉhiššapṭo yeṣe raša'*
>> When he sues, let him be found guilty
> *utᵉpillato tihye laḥᵃṭa'a*
>> Let his verdict be—conviction

The normal sense of *tᵉpilla*, "prayer," will then be a reflex of the verb *hitpallel* whose basic sense is "to seek a judgment for oneself" (confident that God will find for you; for this conative sense of *hitpaʿel*, compare *hithannen* "supplicate," lit. "seek favor for oneself").[2]

We turn now to consider a petitionary speech to a king, with the aim of testing our assertion that the language of prayer follows interhuman speech patterns. Shimei son of Gera, a relative of the ill-starred King Saul, had spitefully abused King David on his flight from Absalom; after Absalom was killed, David returned, triumphant, and Shimei hurried to meet him at the Jordan. He fell prostrate before David and said (2 Sam. 19:20-21):

> *petition:* Let my lord not reckon it against me as an offense, and do not remember how offensively your servant acted on the day my lord the king went out of Jerusalem, or take it to heart;
> *motivation:* for your servant knows that I have sinned, and here I have come today, the first of all the house of Joseph to come down and meet my lord the king.

This is a request for amnesty—quite in the literal sense of Greek *amnēstia*, "oblivion," a term closely related to another Greek word taken over bodily into English, *amnēsia*, "forgetfulness." The petition proper consists of no less than three requests to put Shimei's act out of mind—"not reckon," "not remember," "(not) take to heart." A formal address (e.g., "O my lord, the king!") is lacking, as it usually is in petitions tendered to humans in the Bible. This is explicable by the face-to-face stance of human interlocutors; a pray-er has a need to fix the attention of an invisible God on him by invoking him by name—a need that a man conversing face to face with his fellow does not feel. Accordingly we may well suppose that in reality formal address was an optional element in petitions, and hence not likely to be missed in a literary adaptation. In Shimei's petition, however, another factor is at work: a servile tone bespeaking total submission to David's authority. This dictated peppering the speech with one instance of "my lord," two of "my lord the king," and two of "your servant," determining, in turn, that references to David be deferentially oblique—and thus excluding such confrontational language as invocation in direct address. (The lapses into second person [e.g., "your servant"] are characteristic of this type of deferential speech; compare Judah's speech in Gen. 44:18 ff.). On rare occasions prayers may also be couched in such oblique style—in which case they too lack an invocation—suggesting that the pray-er feels out of favor (see Moses's prayer in Num. 27:15 ff., and note that it follows a reproach).

Having appealed to the relationship of loyal subject to liege lord in his petition, Shimei provides proof of his sincerity in the motivating sentence. He affirms that he is cognizant of his guilt—the expression suggests a more settled consciousness than the regular confessional formula ("I have sinned") soon to be discussed—and points to his alacrity in greeting the king as proof of his sincere reformation. By referring to himself as the first of the Josephides, he identifies himself with a prime royal interest: restoration of Davidic authority over the kingdom, of which, beside Judah, the house of Joseph was the largest and most populous component. If the king pardoned Shimei, who was notorious for having abused him publicly, that would signal a general amnesty of rebellious Joseph as a whole, and, as a matter of course, of rebellious Judah, the king's own tribe; a general reconciliation of the entire kingdom would thereby be greatly facilitated. Shimei's recantation thus offered David an opportunity to win back all of Israel at a stroke, as David immediately grasped; for he rejected Abishai's offer to kill Shimei, exclaiming: "Do I not know that today I am king over Israel?"

We cannot pursue this topic further here, but by way of summary let me say that E. Gerstenberger has carefully studied the Scriptural forms of interhuman petition (*Der bittende Mensch* [Neukirchen-Vluyn, 1980], pp. 17-63). Comparing his results with those I obtained from a full formal study of petitionary prayers shows a marked congruence between the patterns employed by the two.

Shimei's petition contained a confessional element; let us now turn our attention to that speech form, and study its pattern first in an interhuman situation, then in prayer.

During Saul's persecution of David, David twice abstained from exploiting an opportunity to kill Saul, thus showing that he bore him no ill-will. The second time, Saul was overcome with remorse and cried (1 Sam. 26:21):

confession: I have sinned:
petition: return, my son David,
motivation-renunciation: for I shall not harm you again, inasmuch as my life was precious in your eyes today.
acknowledgment of folly: Surely I have acted foolishly and erred very gravely!

The components of this confession derive from the situation of the confessor confronting the person he has injured. The solidarity normally existing between the two has been undone, and the confessor has come to realize that he is at fault. Full of remorse, he seeks to reconcile the injured person; his need is the pardon and goodwill only his fellow can grant. But how can he persuade him to grant it; how can he establish identification between them, on which basis he can appeal to his fellow to bestow the good he possesses? As the first, crucial step he lets him know that he recognizes his guilt. This creates the first link between them—a shared evaluation of the confessor's past behavior as blameworthy. By identifying himself with the injured person's estimate of him, the confessor lays the foundation for the petition that follows. He accomplishes this through uttering the charged word ḥaṭati, "I have sinned." (Many moderns back away from this translation as too religious for an interhuman context, preferring "I am guilty" or the like. This is a reasonable, but not unanswerable stricture; in any event, since my purpose is to show the parallels between the language of these two contexts, I retain the conservative, "wooden" translation for its service to my cause.)

The petition asks for reconciliation: the injured is entreated to end his alienated behavior that was caused by the confessor's now-regretted injury to him. Saul asks David to return to his post at the court, and calls David "my son" to underline his rekindled affection toward him.

In order to motivate the petition, the confessor, on his part, renounces any repetition of his misdeed: this serves as a tender of a good in return for the injured's granting reconciliation; an interest of the injured is appealed to in order to persuade him. Saul adds conviction to his renunciation by spelling out David's right to it: he seals, as it were, his promise to David by acknowledging that David earned it when he refrained from harming Saul though he might have done so with impunity.

Saul closes his speech by stigmatizing his past behavior as folly and gravest error. This resumes the confession and heightens it: not only does the confessor identify himself with the injured person's estimate of his behavior as guilty ("I have sinned"); he divests himself of any vestige of pride by declaring himself to be an erring fool. This is the last word in self-depreciation, all the more trenchant in the mouth of a king. Such total self-exposure, naked of all defenses and claims, is calculated to excite the sympathy of one's fellow, and to encourage his acquiescence in the plea for reconciliation.

A skeleton of the confession-pattern is the message of capitulation that the rebel King Hezekiah sent to his Assyrian overlord Sennacherib, after Sennacherib had captured all the fortified cities of Judah (2 Kings 18:14):

> *confession:* I have sinned;
> *petition:* withdraw from me.
> *motivation-renunciation:* Whatever you impose on me I shall
> bear.

The brevity of this message suggests it is a literary re-working—a summary rather than a transcript. All the more weighty, then, is its formal resemblance to Saul's speech. It opens with the same formula, ḥaṭati, "I have sinned." (It is noteworthy that the Assyrian kings also use "religious" terms of opprobrium when they describe, in their inscriptions, rebels' violations of their divinely sanctioned vassal oaths.)[3] Next it petitions for an end to the results of the misdeed ("withdraw from me"). It motivates the petition by a promise to bear any punitive imposts. Implicitly this is a renunciation of the misdeed, but explicitly it goes beyond it. When verse seven states that Hezekiah rebelled against the king of Assyria "and did not serve him," it means that he stopped paying the levies, taxes, and tribute a vassal king owes his over-lord. The Assyrian, who suffered losses both in material (his army and his treasury) and in prestige (a vassal had dared to rebel), must have been inclined to go beyond merely capturing Judah's towns, in order to recoup on both counts. So it was not enough for Hezekiah to promise to stop his wrongdoing (as Saul did)—in Heze-kiah's case, to resume his payment of tribute. Instead, he offers total submission with readiness to bear any exemplary punishment. This was a good calculated to appeal to the Assyrian's interest—a good for which he might be ready to withdraw his forces without destroy-ing Judah.

The confessionary pattern used by one who wished to reconcile an estranged fellow is precisely that used by man intent upon reconciling God.

A narrative may allude to confessionary prayer by the opening formula alone: "They gathered to Mizpah,

and drew water and poured it out before YHWH, and
they fasted on that day, and they said there, 'We have
sinned [ḥaṭanu] to YHWH'" (1 Sam. 7:6). Solomon's
prayer at the inauguration of the temple envisages
future exiles who would repent and supplicate God,
"saying, 'We have sinned, we have offended, we have
acted wickedly'" (1 Kings 8:47). Such elaboration of the
opening formula is characteristic of late-monarchic and
post-exilic examples of confessionary prayers (e.g.,
Dan. 9:5).

A fuller text occurs in 2 Samuel 24:10—David's confessionary prayer on realizing he sinned by taking a
census:

> *confession:* I sinned gravely in what I did,
> *petition:* and now, YHWH, pray remove the offense of your
>   servant,
> *acknowledgment of folly:* for I have been very foolish.

These components are identical with those found in
interhuman confession. Renunciation is absent—words
to the effect of "I'll never do it again"—but was the likelihood of repeating a census so great that it had to be
formally repudiated? Practically speaking, the acknowledgment of folly includes renunciation, and is all the
more powerful (as was Saul's), seeing that it is spoken
by a king.

A dramatic account of a communal confession, containing dialogue with an angry God, appears in Judges
10:10-15. The Ammonites had been afflicting the apos-
tate Israelites severely; then the Israelites turned to God
in prayer:

confession: We have sinned to you,
(detail:) for we have forsaken our God and worshiped the Baals
—Then YHWH said to the Israelites: "From Egypt, from the Amorites, from the Ammonites, and from Philistines—and when Sidonians and Amalek and Maon oppressed you, and you cried to me, I saved you from their hands. Yet you forsook me and worshiped other gods; so I will not save you any more. Go cry to the gods you have chosen. Let them save you in your time of trouble!"

The Israelites said to YHWH:
confession: We have sinned;
renunciation: you may do to us whatever is good in your eyes,
petition: only rescue us this day!

Apart from God's angry remonstrance (Kimḥi supposes, through a prophet), the pattern is familiar. The detailing of the sin however is new. Not content to draw the curtain of generality over their error, the confessors expose their guilt in detail. By so doing, they demonstrate an awareness of its extent and heinousness, and thus identify themselves with the injured, who is certainly aware of all the painful details. It is just at this point, we note, that God breaks in and gives vent to his vexation in a particularized bill of indictment.

To this demonstration of the parallels between interhuman confession and confessionary prayer, we add, by way of concluding this stage of our inquiry, an inference drawn from a law.

J. Milgrom has drawn attention, in another context, to the requirement of the *'ašam* ritual—the reparation sacrifice expiating a deliberately committed offence—that the ritual and reparation payment must be accompanied by confession: the pertinent law in Numbers 5:7 reads:

> If a man or a woman commits any wrong against a person
> [*ḥaṭ'ot ha'adam*] whereby he trespasses against YHWH, when
> that person feels guilt, he shall confess the wrong [*ḥaṭat-*] he has
> done, make reparation in its entirety.... [following Milgrom,
> *Cult and Conscience* (Leiden, 1976), p. 105]

From the parallel in Leviticus 5:5 f., it appears (argues
Milgrom) that the confession must be performed before
the sacrifice is offered, in all likelihood apart from the
sanctuary and its personnel. For our purpose, it is
remarkable that amidst all the minute particulars into
which the lawmaker goes, the wording of the confession
is not to be found. The lawmaker evidently supposed
that the commoner was capable on his own of formulating it appropriately. What justified such confidence? We
surmise: the practice of modelling confessionary prayer
after the pattern of interhuman confessionary speech—
a simple, natural pattern, corresponding to the dynam-
ics of the transaction and therefore known to everyone.

Our third example of the social analogy of prayer-
speech comes from the expression of gratitude. This
time we shall start from the religious situation, because
the subject of thanksgiving prayer has been so misunder-
stood that O. Eissfeldt, in his standard *The Old Testament: an introduction* (translated by P. Ackroyd
[Oxford, 1965], p. 18), can say that no complete speci-
men of one has survived in the Bible. How then do
Scriptural characters express thanks to God in everyday
circumstances—that is, not by a hymn recited in the
temple (like Hannah in 1 Sam. 2:1 ff.), but in speech
extemporized anywhere? Consider Abraham's servant
at the well in Haran: He has just had his prayer for a
suitable wife for his master's son answered in the person

of Rebeccah—who turns out to be of Abraham's own family. Joyful, the servant bows and prostrates himself before YHWH and says (Gen. 24:27):

> *baruk-formula:* Blessed be YHWH,
> (*epithet:*) God of my lord Abraham,
> *ground:* who has not relinquished his constancy and his fidelity toward my lord:
> (*detail:*) as I was on the way, YHWH led me to the house of my lord's kin.

We learn from this that when biblical man experiences an answer to his prayer, he celebrates it by publicly extemporizing a benediction of God. The juxtaposition of the prayer and its fulfilment is a signal of God's intervention; the happy recipient of divine bounty expresses his gratitude (I know no better word for the feeling) through the benediction. Scriptural characters experience any fortunate turn of events, any unexpected good, any successful issue of a momentous undertaking as a benevolent action of God on their affairs, and their regular, grateful response is by benediction.

The speech of David, whose life is full of lucky turns, offers many examples:

—Grateful to Abigail for dissuading him from massacring Nabal's household, David says (1 Sam. 25:32): "Blessed be YHWH God of Israel who sent you this day to intercept me."

—On receiving news of Nabal's sudden death, David says (1 Sam. 25:39): "Blessed be YHWH, who defended me in the matter of the insult I suffered at the hand of Nabal, and held his servant back from evil. . . ."

—On receiving word on his sickbed that Solomon had been crowned, thus settling the dispute over the succession, the aged David says (1 Kings 1:48): "Blessed be YHWH, God of Israel, who appointed a successor to my throne whom I could see with my own eyes."

This extemporized, public benediction is uniform. It opens with the passive participle *baruk*, "blessed" (i.e., is an object, or bearer, of *b^{e}raka*, "blessing, increase, success"), followed by the subject, YHWH. The relation between the two words is ambiguous. It might be indicative, with the participle qualifying the proper name: "Blessed is YHWH"—a simple eulogizing assertion; it has so been taken by many. But it also might be an optative relation—the expression of a wish, "blessed be YHWH"; and the balance is tilted in favor of the optative by an explicit, longer form found in a benediction by the Queen of Sheba, "May YHWH your God be blessed [*y^{e}hi... baruk*]" (1 Kings 10:9); (this explicit optative is paralleled in the benedictions of humans later to be discussed). The *baruk*-formula is the benediction proper, but in the extemporized situation, it is regularly followed by a complementary relative clause particularizing the happy occasion ascribed to God which evoked the benediction ("who did thus and so"). The whole is a statement about God rather than a speech made to him, and it is intended for others to hear. It is a testimony to the author's perception of the happy event as a gift of God, a testimony gratefully offered in public for the greater glory of God.

But precisely what is the meaning of the *baruk*-formula, which appears to wish a blessing on God? Ancients and moderns alike have been perplexed by the apparent suggestion that God is subject to some external source of enhancement. A solution to this hard question may develop as we pursue our main topic: the analogy between social language and the language of prayer.

How do the characters in the Bible express gratitude among themselves?

A law in Deuteronomy 24:13 requires that a lender who takes a poor man's garment in pledge for a loan must return it at evening, so that the poor man can sleep in his garment, "and," the law concludes, "he will bless you and you will gain merit in the eyes of YHWH your God." Listing his righteous acts, Job says (29:12 f.): "I delivered the poor man who cried for help / The orphan who had no helper; / The blessing of one ready to perish came upon me." The formulation of such blessings of gratitude appears time and again in the book of Ruth. Boaz begins his grateful response to Ruth's appeal that he marry her with a benediction: "Blessed be you before YHWH [*b^eruka 'at l^eYHWH*]" (Ruth 3:10).[4] In 2:19 f. Naomi asks Ruth about her success: "Where have you been gleaning today; where were you working? May your benefactor be blessed!" (here the optative is explicit, *y^ehi . . . baruk*). When Ruth identifies the man, Naomi exclaims gratefully: "Blessed be he before YHWH, because he did not relinquish his constancy toward the living and the dead." Again, David expresses his appreciation of the Jabeshites' heroic retrieval and burial of Saul's corpse by a message beginning: "Blessed be you before YHWH, because you performed this act of loyalty toward your lord. . . ." (2 Sam. 2:5). How closely the form of thanking God is related to the form of thanking man appears in David's juxtaposing them in a single burst of gratitude to Abigail for having kept him from massacre: "Blessed be YHWH God of Israel who sent you to intercept me this day! Blessed be your sense and blessed be you, who restrained me today from incurring bloodguilt and taking the law into my own hands" (1 Sam. 25:32 f.).

The interhuman transaction giving rise to such an expression of gratitude seems clear. A has done B a good turn, B, feeling under obligation (or as we say, obliged) to A, invokes God's blessing on him to discharge this obligation—as it were, making good A's outlay on his behalf. B's benediction follows directly and spontaneously upon his recognition of A's favor. It usually takes the form of a binary sentence—a *baruk l^eYHWH*, "blessed be . . . before YHWH," formula—and a particularization of the favor for which B feels obliged. By spelling out A's kind act, B demonstrates his appreciation of it. A is gratified by this particularized appreciation, over and above the less tangible good wish to which it is attached; B on his part is content to have made a return to A that pleases him.

The elements of such an interhuman transaction can be present up to a point in a transaction between biblical man and God. Since the biblical God is endowed with personality, a benefit from him signals his favor and thus gives rise to a feeling of obligation in the human recipient. He discharges this feeling in a testimonial declaration about God—thus turning the occasion into a public enhancement of God's glory, surely as pleasing to God as it is uplifting to man. Apart from this change to third-person testimonial from second-person address, the formulas of benediction of God and man are analogous; and while that clinches our argument, it leaves us with the above mentioned perplexity regarding the meaning of the optative *baruk YHWH* formula. Put bluntly: of man it can be said, *baruk X l^eYHWH*, "Blessed be X before YHWH"; but when we say *baruk YHWH*, ["before" whom] is YHWH blessed?

A plausible conjecture derives this formula from a

world view in which forces outside of God were thought
to exist, to which he was subject. The pagan gods are
subject to magic and fate, among other forces; similarly,
it is conjectured, Israel's God—like man—was once subject to *b^eraka*, "blessing, increase." As it was possible to
invoke *b^eraka* on a fellow man, so it was possible to
invoke it for the benefit of God.[5] Later, when the biblical nonmythological conception of Israel's God prevailed, the invocation of *b^eraka* on man was often explicitly complemented by *l^eYHWH*, "before YHWH,"
to leave no room for doubt that all *b^eraka* comes from
him. The survival of the phrase *baruk YHWH* can only
be ascribed, in my opinion, to its functional analogy to
the *baruk X* formula used with humans. David's pairing
of *baruk YHWH* and *b^eruka 'at* "blessed be YHWH"
and "blessed be you" shows how natural it was to juxta-
pose the two in one breath; gratitude for a human favor
might readily have been coupled with acknowledgment
that underlying it was the grace of God. Such functional
analogy (serving the expression of gratitude), along
with occasional spoken juxtapositions, were enough to
preserve the original formal parallelism of the two
baruk formulas, even after the one with YHWH as subject was no longer understood in its original sense owing
to the new non-mythological conception of God in biblical religion. How the biblical authors interpreted *baruk
YHWH* can be surmised from the equivalence in hymnal
language of the verbs *berak*, "bless," and *hillel*,
"praise," when the object is God (similarly the cognate
nouns *b^eraka*, "blessing," and *t^ehilla*, "praise," serve as
synonyms); compare, for example, Ps. 34:2; 145:2;
Neh. 9:5. Accordingly, *baruk YHWH* was understood
as "may YHWH be praised"—virtually identical in

meaning with the fuller and explicitly optative expression $y^e hi$ $šem$ $YHWH$ $m^e borak$, "may the name of YHWH be blessed/praised" (Ps. 113:2 [answering the call to praise ($hal^e lu$) God]; Job 1:21; Dan. 2:20 [Aramaic]).

It is time to summarize and conclude. We have seen that several types of prayer are formulated in patterns analogous to those used in the Scriptures for interhuman speech. We have sought to derive these patterns from the social and psychological factors at work in purely human situations of petitioning, confessing, and expressing gratitude. The patterns remain constant throughout the Scriptures, regardless of source, because they arise immediately and naturally from life. Just as no differences contingent on literary sources occur in an interhuman pattern of speech of a given class, so no differences contingent on literary sources occur in a given prayer-pattern. For example: extemporized benedictions of God are of the same pattern throughout the Scriptures, just as extemporized benedictions of man are. This means that the biblical narrators all portrayed speech between man and God on the analogy of speech between humans. Such a procedure accords perfectly with the personal conception of God in the Scriptures; the only analogy available for intercourse with him was the human-personal.

To what extent are the literary representations of both prayer and interhuman speech literary conventions? To some extent we must assume that any literary formulation is attended by some shaping, following conventions of economy, dramatization, heightening by contrast, and so on. But there is no reason for supposing that the principle of portraying popular prayer as extemporized on the analogy of interhuman speech is a literary invention. Why should biblical authors over centuries have placed speeches in the mouths of their characters that had no verisimilitude, not even in principle? Until a plausible ground for doubt is offered, the most probable construction of the literary evidence is as a reflection of a reality in which humans might speak to God as they did to one another—with the same freedom and in the same speech patterns. To be sure, we must reckon with literary shaping of speech in both cases; but having made such allowance, the simplicity and manifest functionality of the patterns of speech and prayer encourage belief that in the embedded prayers we have as faithful a correspondence as we might wish to the form and practice of everyday, nonprofessional, extemporized verbal worship in ancient Israel.

Recently, two serious scholars have, each in a footnote, belittled the significance of the embedded prayers for the understanding of biblical religion, on theoretical grounds. In the next and final lecture in this series, these remarkable positions will be considered. It will then be argued that, on the contrary, these data point to a hitherto unrecognized inwardness of the popular religion of ancient Israel.

LECTURE 3

In the preceding lectures I have argued (1) that the prose prayers of the Bible, represented as extemporized by the laity, follow patterns, whose components arise naturally from the circumstances; and (2) that these patterns are similar to the representation of interhuman speech patterns in analogous circumstances, and that there is no reason to suspect the veridicality of the principle that the laity extemporized prayer on the analogy of social speech.

Granting the validity of these arguments, it may be concluded that in ancient Israel, in principle, anyone could pray. By this I mean that anyone capable of conventional interhuman discourse was capable of praying; equally, that the prayer of anyone was deemed acceptable to God. This conclusion would not seem to justify the trouble taken to arrive at it; it would be impolite, but perhaps not inexcusable, to greet it with, "So what?"

Before the attempt is made to say "what," current scholarly positions on this topic must be aired as the first step in explaining the length at which I have expounded it.

Scholarly appreciation of the embedded prayers in the Hebrew Scriptures has been bedeviled by disabling preconceptions. The arch-devil is the dichotomizing of prayer into spontaneous, free invention on the one hand, and preformulated, prescribed prayers on the other. Y. Kaufmann, easily first among modern Jewish Bible scholars, assessed biblical prose prayers as follows:

> We do not know whether in pre-exilic times fixed prayers were
> current—prayers whose wording was set. Almost all the prayers
> found in the Scriptures belong to specific pray-ers and to specific
> occasions; they spring from the special circumstances in which
> they were composed, hence they have no set wording. A set
> prayer is a composition that has been detached from its author
> and the situation in which it was uttered—detached from an
> individual and his particular need to become a public vehicle of
> expression to serve those who speak not what they think but
> what it is conventional to say. Set prayer is public property, but
> all the prayers of biblical characters are individual and tailored
> for the occasion. (*Toldot ha-'emuna ha-yiśre'elit* II [Tel-Aviv,
> 1946], p. 502)

The scholarly attitude toward the two members of
this dichotomy has changed in the course of time. At the
beginning of this century, the study of prayer was dominated by the magisterial and still indispensable survey
of F. Heiler, *Das Gebet* (5th ed., München/Basel, 1969
[1st ed. 1918], published in English as *Prayer*, trans. by
S. McComb and J. E. Park [London, 1932]). Heiler did
not suppress his romantic Protestant predilection for the
free spirit of the individual. True prayer, he asserted, is
the "original, simple prayer of the heart"; "formal literary prayers are merely [their] weak reflection" (*Prayer*,
p. xviii); set prayer is the impersonal, spiritually desic-
cated, final stage of prayer. As the "link" between true
prayer of the heart and the mechanical set prayer, Heiler
mentions "the flexible, elastic outline, which in a free
way was adapted to the concrete needs of the moment"
(p. 66). But he does not dwell on this transitional or
"intermediate" (*Prayer*, pp. 10 f.) form—of such interest
to us! The degeneration was caused by the "growing
feeling of uncertainty in regard to the divinity . . . which
is set to rest only by fixed formulas," and by "the inabil-
ity for independent expression" (p. 66).

The modern study of society, followed by the even

more modern study of simple cultures brought about a change of opinion reflected in the treatment of biblical prayer after the Second World War. The community came to be appreciated as the matrix of creativity and values. The origin of prayer was now sought in the formal, liturgical prayers of the community; solo praying was performed by an expert who served as the communal spokesman. His creations were subsequently adopted by the individual. Here are three formulations of the modern position. I quote first from S. Mowinckel, *Religion und Kultus* (Göttingen, 1953), p. 121:

> In the development of religion, the liturgical or ritual prayer has played a greater role than "free prayer." In Israel we see remarkably little free prayer outside of cultic occasions and unconnected with a cult place even with the prophets; basically it occurs to a marked extent only with Jeremiah, and to some extent with Amos. But it can be present and lie hidden even under a rigidly prescribed life of prayer, as is the case with the fixed times of prayer and the prescribed formulas of Islam. Precisely Islam shows how the believer can add his own private prayers to the prescribed confession and the laudative ṣalāt! We see the same in Judaism, from Samuel's mother Hannah, who made use of the worship of the festival service to "pour out her heart before the Lord," to the publican in the parable [Luke 18:13], who, when the time for prayer came, could produce nothing other than his "God, be merciful to me a sinner."
>
> The fixed forms constitute no barrier—indeed they are often of help. Even a spontaneous or private prayer can find expression in the prescribed forms of prayer in the service; it has often proved true that what the individual feels in his heart can be better expressed in that than in his own words. Many in the course of time have become increasingly thankful for the help of a life of prayer, which goes to show that one can elicit private and personal prayers from the very order of the service.

Mowinckel not only asserts the priority of set prayer, he apologizes for it—evidently reacting to its denigration

by such as Heiler. Because he does not bestow any attention on the Scriptural "free prayers," he can lump extemporized prayers of individuals (Jeremiah, Amos, and
Hannah) with private meanings that one who recites set
prayers can find in them. He declares free prayer to be a
negligible phenomenon. The evidential value of Hannah's prayer is discounted by representing it as adjunct
to the festival service, as gratuitous an assertion as that
the publican's extemporized prayer was adjunct to the
daily service: the location of both prayers in the temple
is of no consequence for their essentially spontaneous
character. Ignoring the data on the free prayers, Mowinckel adduces the Scriptures to support his generality that
liturgical prayer was a greater factor in shaping religion.

E. Gerstenberger's *Der bittende Mensch*, which I have
already gratefully mentioned, examines the petitions
and complaints of the individual in the Hebrew Scriptures in the light of the Babylonian incantation prayers.
Not surprisingly, Gerstenberger arrives by this route at
the conclusion that the Hebrew petitions and complaints, like the Babylonian incantations, were composed and recited by experts to whom members of the
community resorted to mediate their transactions with
God. The Scriptural texts that Gerstenberger so search-
ingly examines and interprets are all psalms; Gerstenberger's contribution is a new theory of their life-setting,
since, as is notorious, the psalms lack explicit data on
their life-settings. Curiously, while Gerstenberger includes in his study a close analysis of interhuman petitions, he not only fails to examine the petitionary prayers embedded in narratives, he explicitly discounts them:

> It emerges with perfect clarity that, alongside the cultic-cere-
> monial petitions, spontaneous, direct [= unmediated] prayer to

YHWH existed; cf. Gen. 19:17 ff., 20:14 ff.; Judges 15:18, 16:28;
1 Sam. 1:10 ff. Only this "free lay-prayer (A. Wendel, *Das freie
Laiengebet im vorexilischen Israel*, Leipzig, 1931) is rather a reflex (*ein Reflex*) of cultic custom than the other way around."
[P. 135, n. 87]

Unlike Mowinckel, Gerstenberger admits that spontaneous and cultically mediated prayer were coeval; he does
not brush aside the evidence of the former's antiquity.
But his theory that the community's expert prayer-medi-
ator is primary makes him discount the spontaneous
phenomenon as a mere reflex of him; he does not argue
this position.

The most thoroughgoing advocate of the priority of
ritual, set prayer is M. Haran, an expert on the institutions of Israelite worship. In a recent article entitled
"Priest, Temple and Worship" (*Tarbiz* 48 [1978], p.
184), Haran evaluates prayer as follows: Prayer was the
poor man's version of temple-worship; since he could
not afford the only proper tender of homage to God—
animal sacrifice—he offered a prayer in its stead. "He
equipped himself with a ready-made form of prayer,
with set wording, composed by the temple poets; examples of these were later collected in the book of Psalms.
It appears that it was neither appropriate nor respectable
to utter before the Lord in his temple such spontaneous
thoughts as occurred to the pray-er."

Haran has qualified his statement by limiting it to the
temple context; in a footnote to it, however (n. 14), he
gives it general validity:

Similarly for most times and most places, prayer (whose origin
is magical formulas) was a matter of stereotypic phraseology,
and not private thoughts. Such was the case, in any event, in the
history of Israel. I think that the prose prayers that the biblical
authors occasionally put into the mouths of characters, are sus-

ceptible for the most part to the explanation that they are a prose transcription [m^{e}sira, lit. transmission] of an idea content that, in reality, should more appropriately have been uttered in formulaic language and best in the high language of poetry. (Transcription [m^{e}sira] of the gist of the prayer in prose sentences was perhaps easier for the author, and also does not extrude him from the frame of the narrative.) In any event, the biblical data must be adjusted to the general course of the history of prayer, which moves from the fixed stereotype to free prose, and from the formulaic to the spontaneous. Prayer as unmediated thought appears to be a modern phenomenon, whose place is at the end of the process, not at its beginning.

In Mowinckel, Gerstenberger, and Haran we see a reversal of Heiler's position; yet the latter-day scholars share with their predecessor two questionable assumptions. Both Haran and Heiler imagine a linear development of prayer from one stage to another (Heiler speaks of a transition stage, linking the extremes); they differ only on the termini. This runs counter to the biblical evidence for the contemporaneity of all stages of prayer. All four scholars take seriously only two types of prayer: on the one hand, the spontaneous "outpouring of the heart," and, on the other hand, the studied composition of the expert, which might be appropriated for individual, private use. This dichotomy simply does not do justice to the evidence as we have seen it.

It deserves to be noted in passing that such a dichotomy does not adequately account even for the form of early Jewish prayer—which was a far cry from the rigidity it manifests in modern times as a result of the tyranny of the printing press. Here is J. Heinemann's description of the early form:

When the sages ordained the obligatory fixed prayers, they did not prescribe their exact wording—contrary to what is usually

thought and written in popular books on prayer. They prescribed a framework: the number of benedictions comprising
each prayer—such as the eighteen of the week-day 'amida, the
seven of the sabbath and festival, and so forth. They also prescribed the topic of each benediction; for example, in a given
benediction one must ask for the rebuilding of Jerusalem; in
another, for the ingathering of the exiles. But they did not, nor
did they ever seek to, prescribe the wording of any benediction
or any prayer. That was left as a rule to the pray-er—to be
exact, to the prayer-leader [a layman]. ("Fixity and renewal in
Jewish prayer" [Hebrew], in G. Cohen, ed., *Ha-tefilla ha-
yehudit, hemšek ve-ḥidduš* [Ramat-Gan: 1978], pp. 79 f.; for
further detail, see J. Heinemann, *Prayer in the Talmud* [Berlin,
New York, 1977], pp. 37-69)

At bottom, this dichotomy fails to appreciate the mix-
ture of spontaneity and prescription in all social behavior (and prayer, as we have argued, is social behavior)
—particularly in a traditional society. From our own
observations we can attest to the wide extent of pattern-
ing in our verbal behavior in sensitive situations: formulas of greeting and taking leave; polite yet noncom-
mittal personal inquiry and the prescribed retorts there-
to; a hortatory address to a bar-mitzvah boy; conduct-
ing patter at a reception. Conventions govern openings
and closings, and the proper contents. Such conventions
are what enable every cultured person to play his
momentary role by filling the empty lines of the pattern
with substance tailored to the situation. They make
spontaneity possible precisely because they free the individual from the burden of sizing up the varied situations
that come his way and deciding on the spot what appropriate components of discourse, what topics, are dictated by them. The components are supplied by the conventions attached to the situation; it falls to the individual to infuse the specific content into them according to

circumstances. The extemporized prayers of the Bible
require little more capacity than we can observe in our-
selves; and this little more is accounted for easily by the
traditionality of biblical society. Rural American Protes-
tants at grace can equal in inventiveness most biblical
characters at prayer; and the average Arab peasant is
probably as adept as David was in extemporizing blessings (and curses). There is something between set ritual
prayers and free invention; it is the patterned prayer-
speech that we have been describing.

"Between" does not mean a point on an evolutionary
line between two temporal termini, but a level of speech
between others that any speaker might choose at a given
time. A visit to a temple—not an everyday occurrence
—called for care, thoughtfulness, and perfection in expression that a commoner could supply only by recourse
to a temple-poet's prepared text. Such were the psalms;
the devout commoner could reach for such tender and
profound religious sentiments under the impact of a
visit to the temple, but he could never adequately articu-
late them on his own, and so happily adopted another's
expert formulation of them. That is the solid kernel of
truth in Haran's position. But sometimes even at a temple, and regularly outside it, our data show that any
Israelite might pray on impulse without recourse to prepared texts. Such praying is spontaneous in that it
springs from an occasion and its content is freely tailored to circumstances. At the same time it conforms to
a conventional pattern of more or less fixed components
(topics) appearing in a more or less fixed order. Beside
these, a third level of prayer is attested—the totally un-
conventional and artless. It might be little more than an
exclamation, such as David's "O frustrate Ahitophel's

counsel, YHWH!" (2 Sam. 15:31), or it might be phrased
like an expostulation with a familiar, such as Samson's:
"You have granted this great victory by the hand of
your servant; now shall I die of thirst and fall into the
hands of these uncircumcised?!" (Judg. 15:18). These
answer to Heiler's "original outpourings of the heart,"
though they are not particularly inspired or inspiring.

These three levels of praying were coeval, and one
and the same biblical character is attested as praying on
more than one of them. Hannah is said to have extemporized a long prayer on one occasion (1 Sam. 1:12), and
on another, she recites a thanksgiving psalm (1 Sam. 2:
1-10). Samson expostulates formlessly on one occasion
(Judg. 15:18), but later he carefully follows a conventional petitionary pattern (Judg. 16:28). One of David's
prayers is a one-line exclamation (2 Sam. 15:31), but he
also extemporizes patterned petitions, confessions, and
benedictions; furthermore, he is famous for composing
highly stylized poems and psalms. King Hezekiah, fallen
sick, extemporizes a brief prose prayer of petition;
healed, he dedicates a written psalm (*miktab*) of thanksgiving to God (Isa. 38:2 f., 9-20). Nothing warrants setting up an evolution, starting at either end of this ladder
of prayer. All three levels were available throughout the
period of biblical literature, and narrators might choose
to place their characters on any level according to circumstances. Not only can anyone pray in the Bible, but
anyone may pray on any level of prayer—though to be
sure, only experts can compose prayers of the highest
technical and ideational level (psalms).

Study of the narrative art of the Scriptures has something to gain from attention to the embedded prose
prayers. Because the embedded prayers are tailored to

their circumstances, they can serve to delineate character—as in reality we may believe that, since extemporized prayer gave scope to individuality, a person was
revealed by his prayers. The transcendent background
of events may be brought to the fore by the presence of
prayer, as the absence of prayer may suppress it: the
adventures of Joseph and of Esther and Mordechai give
ample occasion for prayer and benediction; their total
absence in both narratives helps lend each its secular
quality—all mundane foreground with action motivated
by human passions. To the contrary, the story of
David's career, filled with intrigue and a full range of
worldly passions, is touched with sublimity, owing to
its hero's constant resort to prayer, by which he attributes to God all his fortunes, good and bad. (Not for
nothing is David so frequently called—by God as well
as the narrators—"the servant of YHWH" [24 times,
second only to Moses who is so denoted 31 times], and
considered author of many psalms.)

Reference has already been made to the difference
between the high level of artistry and technical finish of
professionally composed prayers (the psalms) and the
simplicity of commoners' extemporizations. The patterns of psalm-composition, thoroughly examined and
described in H. Gunkel and J. Begrich, *Einleitung in die
Psalmen* (Göttingen, 1933) must be compared with
those of the prose prayers; similarly the language, style,
and phraseology must be examined, to determine both
the differences and the possible influences of the one on
the other.[1]

What are the religious implications of the fact that in
principle anyone can pray and be heard by God? Perhaps the most obvious implication is to mark off biblical

prayer decisively from the rigid formulas of magic and incantation (from which scholars regularly derive it). When, as we have seen, the lawmaker prescribes that the reparation-sacrifice must be preceded by confession, but omits fixing its wording, he implies that effective prayer is not a matter of a particular verbal formula. In order to appreciate the significance and singularity of this omission, one needs to be familiar with, say, Babylonian exorcism rituals, whose offerings are accompanied by verbally fixed incantation prayers, or the Roman requirement that prayer be punctiliously performed, since a single mistake would invalidate it.[2] Taken together with the abundant evidence for extemporized popular praying, we conclude that the lawmaker only reflects popular religion in holding the essence of prayer to be its message content, not its wording; the patterns we have discerned merely facilitated extemporization, they did not dictate verbal content. Like interhuman speech, the effectiveness of prayer was not primarily conditioned by wording, but on the total configuration of interpersonal factors. Among these, the moral status of the speaker in the estimate of the one addressed, and his sincerity, play a crucial role.

Biblical Hebrew uses *leb*, "heart," and *nepeš*, "self," (often translated as "soul") to express sincerity (compare with English "wholehearted, whole-souled"). Delilah complains that Samson has been toying with her in repeatedly misleading her about the true source of his strength: "How can you say 'I love you' when your heart is not with me"—that is, your speech has been insincere (Judg. 16:15). Prov. 23:7 describes the miserly host thus: "'Eat and drink' he will say, but his heart is not with you"—his profession is insincere.

Sincerity is a condition of worshiping the biblical God. Samuel lays it down as a requirement of true repentance: "If with all your hearts you are returning to YHWH, remove the alien gods from your midst, and the Ashtoreths, and direct your hearts toward [*hakinu . . . 'el*] YHWH and serve him alone . . . ." (1 Sam. 7:3). Hannah explained herself to the priest Eli, who took the voiceless motion of her lips for a sign of drunkenness, as follows: "Nay, sir, I am an unfortunate woman; I have drunk neither wine nor strong drink, but have been pouring out my soul [*napši*] before YHWH . . . ." (1 Sam. 1:15). We speak of pouring out our guts to someone and mean the same: to expose one's innermost being, revealing its secret concerns without reservation, without withholding anything—to speak all that is in one's mind with utter sincerity and candor.

References to the involvement of the heart in prayer occur even more frequently in the "higher" literature of the Bible—the prophetic, poetic and wisdom books. Lamentations 2:19 calls on Fair Zion to "pour out her heart like water before YHWH"—a simile that has been plausibly invoked to explain the peculiar rite performed at the revival meeting convoked by Samuel for the repentant Israelites: "they drew water and poured it out before YHWH" (1 Sam. 7:6); if this is a correct combination, it shows how commonplace the notion was that prayer meant baring one's insides to God. Here are two of many Psalm allusions to sincerity as the essence of true prayer: "YHWH is near to all who call on him—to all who call on him sincerely" (*be'emet*, lit. "in genuineness"; Ps. 145:18). Condemning the Israelites' hypocritical prayer during the Wilderness wandering, another psalm puts it thus:

When he killed them, they besought him;
They again entreated God.
They recalled that God was their rock,
That God Most High was their redeemer.
They blandished him with their mouths,
With their tongues they lied to him,
But their hearts were not directed toward him [*nakon 'immo*],
They were not faithful to his covenant. (78:34-37)

One of Job's friends, Zophar, commends righteous conduct to him; among its elements is a sincere disposition
of the heart before prayer: "If you have directed your
heart [*haʿkinota libbeka*], then outspread your hands to
him [in prayer]...." (Job 11:13). The prophet Hosea
blames the wicked for insincere prayer, "They did not
shout to me with their hearts when they wailed on their
beds" (7:14). Isaiah expressed God's contempt for hol-
low prayer (29:13):

For this people approaches me with its mouth;
With their lips they reverence me,
But their hearts are far from me;
Thus their religion [lit. fear of me]
Is a duty learned by rote [lit. a learned commandment of men].

The requirement of sincerity in prayer derives from
its social nature as a transaction between persons. One
affects another person not so much by a form of words
as by the spirit that is perceived to animate them. No
wording of an appeal can persuade, when the one to be
persuaded mistrusts the appellant. Since extemporized
prayer puts no store by a prescribed wording, the basis
of its acceptance by God—of God's being touched by it
—must be the sincerity of the professions made by the
pray-er.

Now it is true that most of the allusions to sincerity as

a condition of prayer are to be found in the "high" literature of the Scriptures. The idea that the essence of
prayer is the conformity of speech with thought surely
reflects a refined spirituality. Yet I venture to suggest
that the natural origin of this conception was not in the
professional liturgical poet, or the prophet or sage with
their literary cultivation and sophistication; not in these
whose culture would lead them to prize formal, artistic,
and stylistic values—what we would call "the magic of
words"—but rather in the popular experience of extemporized prayer, the spontaneous, heartfelt reponse to
God's presence or action. It was from the realm of popular values, where the social ideal of sincerity in interpersonal transactions was applied naturally to relations
with God, that prophets, psalmists, and sages, the refin-
ers of religious sentiment, adopted this virtue into their
repertoire of demand and critique.[3]

We have arrived at what is perhaps the most signifi-
cant consequence of the fact that in ancient Israel anyone could pray and be heard.

If indeed the Israelite Everyman resorted freely to
prayer whenever need, gratitude or admiration moved
him—as our sources attest—we must surmise that,
given his religious outlook and the abundance of occasions, he prayed repeatedly. That, in turn, sustained in
his consciousness the vivid reality of God's presence.
Without extemporized prayer as his habit, the commoner's realization of the transcendent must have faded
(bear in mind that obligatory prayer was unknown in
biblical times, and the temple worship was a daily affair
only of the priesthood). We have only to look at the
secular, prayerless scene about us to see how, in the
absence of an orientation toward the transcendent,

mundane concerns take sole possession of the field of consciousness. Only the accessibility of God through prayer everywhere and at all times and to all persons, ensured the permanent link of the commoner to the transcendent realm. Not only a Rachel, a Leah, or a Hannah, but any distressed wife could "direct her heart" to God and "pour out her soul to him." Not only David, but any father could pray for his sick baby. Not only Jacob could pray to be delivered from a personal enemy, not only Hezekiah could pray to be healed from his disease, but every man and woman. As Solomon puts it with respect to extemporized prayer in the temple, God accepts "any prayer, any supplication which any man of all your people Israel shall have, each of whom knows his own personal affliction" [lit. the affliction of his heart] (1 Kings 8:38).

Constant familiar intercourse with God, unmediated by priest or other ritual expert could only have strengthened the egalitarian tendency (a tendency verging on anarchy) that was rooted in Israel's self-conception. The express purpose of God in offering to make Israel his covenanted people is to convert them into his "kingdom of priests, a holy nation" (Exod. 19:6)—that is, a holy commonwealth in which all members enjoy priestlike intimacy with God. One practical effect of this ideal is to apply to the commoner a standard of conduct proper in the first instance to priests only: the prohibition of eating carrion in Exodus 22:30 is grounded on the admonition to be "people holy to YHWH," the general ground repeatedly given for the special restrictions of the priesthood (e.g., Lev. 21:6); the mutilations associated with mourning are banned to priests, on the ground of their holiness (v. 5)—the same are banned to Israelites at large, and on the same express ground, "for you are a people holy to YHWH your God" (Deut. 14:1 f.). Moses declined young Joshua's urging to imprison Eldad and Medad for having prophesied apart from contact with Moses's spirit, with the generous wish, "Would that all the people of YHWH were prophets, that YHWH set his spirit [not mine!] on them!" (Num. 11:29). In the tale of Korah's rebellion, this ideal is transmuted into an anarchic slogan that may well have threatened more than one leader's authority: "Enough of you! for all the community are holy, every one of them, since YHWH is in their midst; why then do you exalt yourselves above YHWH's congregation?" (Num. 16:3). Exemplary punishment was dealt out to Korah and his followers. But the germ of anarchy never died in Israel. Moses's generous wish is echoed in a prediction of the prophet Joel concerning the last days (3:1 f.):

It shall come to pass afterward,
That I will pour out my spirit upon all flesh;
Your sons and your daughters shall prophesy;
Your old men shall dream dreams,
And your young men shall see visions.
On servants and maids too I will pour out my spirit,
In those days.

Coming down to earth, the unique institution of the synagogue in early Judaism—whose leaders were laymen and whose rich life of prayer lay wholly outside the realm of temple and priesthood—was the consummation of the egalitarian tendency of the Scriptures in spiritual matters. Can there be a doubt that extemporized lay prayer in biblical times played a crucial role in preparing the way for it?[4]

I should like, finally to consider the role that popular prayer may have played in preparing the ground for a major doctrine of classical prophecy—the primacy of morality over forms of worship in God's assessment of Israel.[5] For a praying people, who understood nearness to God in terms of nearness to man, the prophetic teaching, that in order to enjoy God's favor one must identify with him in conduct harmonious with his attributes, cannot have been altogether surprising. In social relations like appeals to like; can it be other in relation to God?

Since it was "the way of YHWH to do what is right and just" (Gen. 18:19), the wisdom writers had already concluded that an evil person had no prospect of gaining a hearing for his prayers. Says the sage of Proverbs 15:29: "YHWH is far from the wicked, but he accepts the prayer of the righteous." The point is repeated by Job's friends:

> If you seek God zealously,
> And make supplication to the Almighty—
> If you are pure and honest,
> Then he will protect you
> And keep your righteous home intact. (8:5 f.)

Again, the conditions of prayer are listed thus:

> If you have directed your heart,
> Then outspread your hands to him;
> If evil is in your hand—remove it,
> And let no iniquity dwell in your tent.... (11:13 f.)

The prophets carried this doctrine to an extreme in their denunciation of Israel's entire worship as hateful to God. Amos thundered in God's name (5:21 ff.):

> I hate, I despise your feasts,
> I will not accept your assemblies;
> If you give me whole offerings,
> And your meal offerings I will not accept,
> Nor will I look at your fattened peace-offerings.
> Take away from me the din of your songs;
> I will not listen to the melody of your lyres.
> But let justice flow like water
> And righteousness like a powerful stream.

Isaiah fulminated (1:11 ff.):

> What do your many sacrifices mean to me, says YHWH?
> I am sated with offerings of rams;
> Suet of fattened bulls, and blood of oxes, and sheep and goats I
>   do not desire . . .
> Your new moons and sabbaths I thoroughly hate;
> They are a burden to me; I cannot bear it.
> And when you spread your hands I will look away from you;
> Even if you pray much, I will not listen to you;
> Your hands are full of blood!

This vehement, unconditional repudiation of the whole of Israel's established worship has several premises: first, that in all its forms, worship is, like prayer, a social transaction between persons, with no magical virtue or intrinsic efficacy. It is rather a gesture of submission and like all gestures a formality whose meaning depends ultimately on the total moral evaluation the recipient makes of the one who gestures; for the recipient to esteem the gesturer there must be some moral identification between them. (I should regard a gesture of good will made to me by my sworn enemy as a trick.) For worship to find favor in God's eyes, the worshiper must identify himself with ("know" in the biblical idiom; e.g., Jer. 22:15 f.) God in the one way possible for man —by imitating his moral conduct (compare also Hos.

4:1 f. and Jer. 9:23). Gestures of submission made by
villains are an abomination to God. This prophetic evaluation of worship as a gesture, and as such contingent
for its value on moral conduct, which is true identification with God, has justly won general admiration; but it
also should excite wonder at and about the spirituality
of the society that served as its matrix.

For classical prophecy was as much a social as an
individual phenomenon; it cannot be conceived apart
from the populace to which it was addressed and which
it was designed to affect. The classical prophets were
not a creative elite patronized by nobles and oligarchs;
on the contrary, they were political and cultural dis-
senters, who bypassed the aristocracy in order to
address the people. The little evidence that we can mus-
ter indicates that they did carry their message to the
people, and the people, sometimes in crowds, listened.
(Only their popularity can explain why an Amos or a
Jeremiah were suppressed by the state as public men-
aces.) Prophetic rhetoric of admonition presupposes
common ground on which prophet and audience stand,
not only regarding historical traditions but religious
demands as well. The prophets seem to appeal to their
audience's better nature, confronting them with demands of God that they know (or knew) but wish to
ignore or forget; as though by thundering they could
awaken their slumbering consciences. There is more
than a little optimism underlying the generations-long
succession of reforming prophets; it reflects the prophets' confidence that, in the final analysis, they had advo-
cates in the hearts of their audience.

Religious and spiritual primitives could not have
understood their message, much less have furnished a

seedbed in which it could grow. Some degree of spiritual enlightenment must be supposed to account for the overall tolerance, even receptivity, of the people; though they refused to comply with the prophets' uncompromising demands, and occasionally persecuted one or another of them, as a rule they allowed them to preach, and even spawned devotees who reverently preserved their speeches until canonization. Unsupported by power and wealth, the classical prophets can have persisted for centuries only because they were rooted in loamy spiritual soil. The populace constituting that soil deserves to be appreciated no less than the exotic flowers that towered above them.

What was the spiritual loam that prepared Israel's soil so that prophecy could thrive in it? Any answer to this question must give due consideration to the popular life of prayer. For it was in extemporized praying that the Israelites experienced a nonmagical approach to God in which form was subordinate to content; here, in immediate contact with a God who "searched the conscience and the heart" (Jer. 11:20; cf. Ps. 7:10), they were sensitized to sincerity in self-disclosure to God; and, finally, it was in prayer that they had constantly to face the issue of adjusting their ways to God's in order to obtain his favor.[6]

If the implications I have drawn from the conclusions of these lectures are true even only in some measure, it is enough to justify pursuing further study of this many-sided topic of endless fascination. For, to a student of the Hebrew Scriptures, what can match the excitement of following a clue that promises to shed new light on the cause of ancient Israel's spiritual distinction and the vitality of its Scriptures down to our time?

NOTES

LECTURE 1

1. On this essential feature of religion, see the pithy essay by W. C. Smith, "Religion as Symbolism," in *The New Encyclopaedia Britannica* (15th ed.): *Propaedia* (Chicago, 1981), pp. 498-500.

2. This point is elaborated by Y. Kaufmann, in *The Religion of Israel: From its Beginnings to the Babylonian Exile* (Chicago, 1960), pp. 93-101.

3. The following prayer texts have been identified (outside of Psalms; references are to the Hebrew text):

A. Passages in which ad hoc prayer is only mentioned.

(1) Gen. 20:7, 12; (2) 25:21; (3) 30:6, 22; (4) 47:31 (see Targum Onk.); (5) Exod. 2:23-24 (cf. Num. 20:16; Deut. 26:7; 1 Sam. 12:8); (6) Exod. 9:29, 33 (cf. 10:16, 18); (7) 14:10; (8) 14:15; (9) 22:22; (10) Lev. 9:24; (11) 16:21; (12) 26:40; (13) Num. 11:2; (14) 21:7; (15) Deut. 9:20; (16) Judg. 3:9 (cf. 4:3; 6:6); (17) 1 Sam. 1:10, 12-15; (18) 7:5; (19) 7:8-9; (20) 8:6; (21) 8:18; (22) 12:17-18; (23) 12:19, 23; (24) 15:11; (25) 2 Sam. 6:18; (26) 12:16; (27) 21:1; (28) 1 Kings 13:6; (29) 18:42 (cf. James 5:18); (30) 2 Kings 4:33; (31) Isa. 42:2-4; (32) 56: 7; (33) Jer. 21:2 (cf. 37:3, 6); (34) Ezek. 22:30; (35) Lam. 3:8, 44; (36) Dan. 2:18; (37) 6:11; (38) Ezra 8:21-23; (39) Neh. 2:4; (40) 4:3; (41) 1 Chron. 5:20; (42) 21:26; (43) 2 Chron. 33:12-13.

B. Passages in which the wording of ad hoc prayers appears.

(1) Gen. 17:18; (2) 18:23-32; (3) 19:18-19; (4) 24:11-14; (5) 24:26-27; (6) 28:3-4; (7) 29:35; (8) 30:24; (9) 32:10-13; (10) 43:14; (11) 48: 15-16; (12) Exod. 4:13; (13) 5:22-23; (14) 17:4; (15) 18:9; (16) 32:11-13; (17) 32:31-32; (18) Num. 11:11-15; (19) 12:13; (20) 14:13-19; (21) 16:15; (22) 16:22; (23) 22:34; (24) 27:16-17; (25) Deut. 1:11; (26) 3:23-25; (27) 9:25-29; (28) Josh. 7:6-9; (29) 7:25; (30) 10:12 (cf. v. 14); (31) Judg. 5:24; (32) 6:36-37, 39; (33) 10:10, 15; (34) 13:8; (35) 15:18; (36) 16:23-24; (37) 16:28; (38) 21:2-3; (39) 1 Sam. 7:6; (40) 12:10; (41) 25:32; (42) 2 Sam. 3:29, 39; (43) 7:18-29; (44) 12:13; (45) 14:17; (46) 15:31; (47) 18:28; (48) 24:3; (49) 24:10; (50) 24:17; (51) 1 Kings 1:36; (52) 1:47; (53) 3:6-9; (54) 8:15-21; (55) 8:22-53;

(56) 8:47; (57) 8:55-61; (58) 10:9; (59) 17:20, 21; (60) 18:36-37; (61) 19:4; (62) 2 Kings 6:17; (63) 6:18; (64) 6:20; (65) 19:15-19; (66) 20:2-3; (67) Jer. 3:22-25; (68) 4:10 = 14:13; (69) 7:16 = 11:14 = 14:11; (70) 14:7-9; (71) 14:19-22; (72) 15:15-18; (73) 16:19; (74) 17: 14-18; (75) 18:19-23; (76) 20:7-13; (77) Ezek. 9:8 (cf. 11:13); (78) Amos 7:2, 7; (79) Jon. 1:14; (80) 9:2; (81) Ruth 1:8-9; (82) 2:4; (83) 2:12; (84) 4:11; (85) 4:14; (86) Dan. 2:19-23; (87) 9:4-19; (88) Ezra 9:6-15; (89) Neh. 1:4-11; (90) 3:36; (91) 5:19 (cf. 6:14; 13: 14, 22, 29, 31); (92) 1 Chron. 4:10; (93) 29:10-19; (94) 2 Chron. 13: 14-15; (95) 14:10; (96) 20:5-12; (97) 30:18-19.

The terminology, definitions, and formal characteristics that underlie these identifications are set forth in my article *"t^{e}filla,"* in *Enṣiqlopedia Miqra'it* viii (Jerusalem, 1981), cols. 896-922. The most weighty study of some of the data remains A. Wendel, *Das freie Laiengebet im vorexilischen Israel* (Leipzig, 1932), even after J. W. Corvin, "A Stylistic and Functional Study of the Prose Prayers of the Old Testament," Ph.D. diss. (Emory University, 1972), Ann Arbor. E. G. Newing's 1978 dissertation (University of St. Andrew's, Scotland, made available to me by courtesy of the author), "The Prose Lamentations of Pre-Exilic Israel," contains detailed exegetical, contextual, stylistic and rhetorical observations; its form-critical focus proves, in the end, unrewarding. The question of extemporized prayer does not come up for separate treatment or evaluation in any of the aforementioned works.

4. For the importance of identification, and an orientation in current study of rhetoric, see "Rhetoric in philosophy: the new rhetoric," in the article Rhetoric, *The New Encyclopaedia Britannica: Macropaedia*, vol. 15, 803-805 (by C. Perelman).

5. In 1 Kings 18:24, Elijah says to the priests of Baal, "You shall call the name of (i.e., pray to) your God and I shall call the name of YHWH. . . ." It may be inferred from this that both the custom of opening petitionary prayers by uttering the name of God, and the phrase "call the name of YHWH" which by synecdoche means "pray" (e.g., Ps. 116:3 f.), originated in the need to distinguish YHWH from other gods (cf. the Hittite prayers collected in J. B. Pritchard, *Ancient Near Eastern Texts relating to the Old Testament* [Princeton: 1969], pp. 393 ff.). Even after monotheism prevailed, this established form of opening petitionary prayers persisted, but with presumably altered significance. On the surface, it was the way in which the pray-er made contact with (he might have thought: fixed the attention of) the invisible God. On a psychological level, it

marked the pray-er's entry into the awareness of being in God's presence; henceforth the pray-er's heart was Godward.

6. It is G. E. Mendenhall's merit to have shown the inadequacy of "a/re/venge/ance" as definitions of *nqm* (*The Tenth Generation* [Baltimore and London, 1973], pp. 69-104). His own attempt at definition embraces "Imperium," "vindicatio," defeat, punish, save, redress, ultimately "paganizing" into avenge. His philology is dominated by his theopolitical dogma that "God [does not] delegate to any political institution sovereignty over persons, and all law can do is merely define (and therefore in part create) evil" (101). Under the scythe of this dogma all contrary evidence falls, as Mendenhall cuts a swathe through the varied ideational fields of Scripture.

7. That the heathen sailors follow the pattern of Israelite prayer is noteworthy, and suggests either that the author ascribed to them a peculiarly Israelite practice, or, on the contrary, that he recognized that extemporized lay prayer was not peculiar to Israel. Evidence of such prayers in the ancient east from outside of Israel is very meager. The surviving documents on religion stem for the most part from royal scribal and priestly circles and reflect learned literary traditions and the world of court and temple. For Mesopotamia, A. L. Oppenheim argued that "the common man . . . remains an unknown, the most important unknown element in Mesopotamian religion" (*Ancient Mesopotamia*, revised edition, completed by E. Reiner [Chicago, 1977], p. 181). On extemporized prayer, W. von Soden writes: "Men must surely have directed formless, free prayer to their gods constantly, whether brief ejaculatory prayers or somewhat longer ones. Only very little of this is transmitted to us in the literature. In the royal inscriptions, for example, it was evidently regarded as contrary to normal style to represent the wording of prayers made in difficult battle situations. At most the fact of praying is mentioned; otherwise a short summary of the content is given" (see "Gebet," in E. Ebeling, B. Meissner, eds., *Reallexikon der Assyriologie*, vol. III [Berlin, 1957-1971], 163). Royal prayers embedded in battle narratives appear in D. D. Luckenbill, *Ancient Records of Assyria and Babylonia*, Vol. II (Chicago, 1927 [reprint, 1968], sections 134, 153, 156 [Sargon]). Inscriptions of Assurbanipal give the wording of free prayers (see Luckenbill, sections 785 [short] and 858-859 [long]). Free prayers of the mother of Nabonidus appear in J. B. Pritchard, ed., *Ancient Near Eastern Texts relating to the Old Testament*, 3d ed. (Princeton, 1969), p. 560. In the epical material, heroes and divinities are often depicted as praying (Pritchard, pp. 80-84, 88

[Gilgamesh]; 114, 117 [Etana]; 106 [Atrahasis]. Very few representations of extemporized prayer have been preserved in Egyptian literature. The younger brother, in the Tale of the Two Brothers, makes a brief petition, in biblical style, in a desperate situation (Pritchard, p. 24); Ramses II, in a battle emergency, makes a long "spontaneous" prayer (M. Lichtheim, *Ancient Egyptian Literature*, Vol. I [Berkeley, 1976], 65 ff.). A good description of the evidence is given by H. Brunner in the article "Gebet," in W. Helck ed., *Lexikon der Aegyptologie*, Vol. II (Wiesbaden, 1977), cols. 452-459. R. Lebrun, *Hymnes et prières hittites* (Louvain la Neuve, 1980), pp. 18 and 55 notes expressly that surviving Hittite prayer texts reflect the milieus of scribes and priests, and leaves out of account, for lack of evidence, the more popular and spontaneous prayers.

This survey (in which I was kindly helped on the Egyptological side by John Baines, Irena Shirun and Miriam Lichtheim) suffices to show that the biblical depiction of the heathen sailors extemporizing a prayer is not without foundation in extrabiblical sources. Yet the evidence is too meager to enable us either to discern the patterns of such prayers or their prevalence among commoners. While much of biblical literature may also have originated among learned circles (see the speculative but highly suggestive monograph of A. Lemaire, *Les écoles et la formation de la Bible dans l'ancient Israël* [Göttingen, 1981]), its orientation toward the people and its critical distance from its characters—aspects of its hortatory and pedagogic tendency—make its portraits even of royalty revealing of elemental features common to all men.

LECTURE 2

1. This analysis derives from the meticulous, well-documented, illuminating discussion of *"das alltägliche Bittschema"* in E. S. Gerstenberger, *Der bittende Mensch*, Wissenschaftliche Monographien zum alten und neuen Testament, 51 (Neukirchen-Vluyn, 1980), pp. 17-63.

2. In this understanding of *t^epilla* and *hitpallel*, I follow I. Goldziher, *Abhandlungen zur arabischen Philologie* 1 (1896), pp. 35-36; S. H. Blank, *Hebrew Union College Annual* 21 (1948), pp. 337 f. n. 12; E. A. Speiser, *Journal of Biblical Literature* 82 (1963), pp. 301-306; I. Seeligmann, *Hebräische Wortforschung* (W. Baumgartner Festschrift), Supplements to Vetus Testamentum 16 (Leiden, 1967),

pp. 277 f. For Ps. 109:7, see *The Writings (Kethubim): a new translation of the Holy Scriptures* (Philadelphia: Jewish Publication Society
of America, 1982), p. 148: "may he be tried and convicted; / may he
be judged and found guilty."

3. See, for example, the inscriptions of Ashurbanipal translated in
Pritchard, *Ancient Near Eastern Texts*, pp. 294 col. a, 295 col a, 297
ff., especially 300 col a.

4. The *lᵉ* in *baruk lᵉ* is commonly explained as indicating cause or
agency, and translated "by" (archaic: "of"; see *Gesenius' Hebrew
Grammar*, ed. by E. Kautzsch and A. E. Cowley [Oxford, 1910]; §
121 f. [p. 389]). New light is shed on the formula from Arad Inscription n. 16, lines 2 f.: *brktklyhwh = beraktika lᵉYHWH*, which T.
Muraoka plausibly renders in the sense, "I entreat of YHWH blessing
upon you," comparing *lᵉ* with the *'el* of "they praised her *'el* (to =
before) Pharaoh" (Gen. 12:15); Targum Neofiti *qdm* "before"); see
Annual of the Japanese Biblical Institute 5 (1979), pp. 92-94. Accordingly, *baruk... lᵉYHWH* = "blessed before YHWH," as indeed Targum renders it in 1 Sam. 15:13; 23:21; 2 Sam. 2:5 (*qdm*). Another
example of the formula found in the Arad inscription occurs in Z.
Meshel, *Kuntilat Ajrud* (Jerusalem: Israel Museum, 1978), opposite
plate 10; Aramaic examples in J. Fitzmyer, *Journal of Biblical Literature* 93 (1974), p. 215; see also J. Naveh, *Bulletin of the American
Schools of Oriental Research* 235 (1979), pp. 28 f.

5. On the conception of making a return to God through blessing
him, see S. Blank, "Some Observations Concerning Biblical Prayer,"
Hebrew Union College Annual 32 (1961), pp. 75-90, esp. pp. 87-90.

LECTURE 3

1. Late prose prayers have been thought to show influence of the
psalms: "Imitation of the psalms and of cultic poetry upon the whole
is also to be noticed in the prayers of later prose-literature, e.g., the
prayer of Solomon... I Ki. 8, the confessions of sin in Ezra 9 and
Neh. 9" (A. Bentzen, *Introduction to the Old Testament*, Vol. I
[Copenhagen, 1948], 165). Such a view must be reconsidered if the
authenticity (the verisimilitude) of extemporized prose prayers in the
earlier literature is admitted. The later prose prayers will then rather
be literary-liturgical elaborations of and expansions upon established prose patterns—with a good deal of Deuteronomic ideology
and language (see M. Weinfeld, *Deuteronomy and the Deuteronomic*

School [Oxford, 1972], pp. 32-45, and the pertinent references in the Scripture index to the section on Deuteronomic phraseology).

2. Babylonian examples are conveniently at hand in R. I. Caplice, *The Akkadian Namburbi Texts*, Sources and Monographs: Sources from the Ancient Near East, I/1 (Los Angeles, 1974). For the Roman view that for prayer to be answered it must be "such as the authorities of the State have laid down as the right wording, and if the ritual accompanying it is equally in order," see W. W. Fowler, *The Religious Experience of the Roman People* (London, 1922), pp. 185-190 (the quotation is on p. 189).

3. Later mishnaic Hebrew *Kiwwen* (*'et halleb*) and its cognate noun *kawwana*(*t halleb*)—technical terms for devout intention and attention in the performance of religious duties—are descended both etymologically (from the root *kwn*) and semantically from the biblical term *hekin leb* (*nakon leb*), "direct the heart (have one's heart directed, devoted)"; this was pointed out by H. G. Enelow, in his *Selected works*, Volume IV, privately printed, 1935, pp. 256 ff.; see also M. Kadushin, *Worship and Ethics* (Evanston, Ill.: Northwestern University Press, 1964), p. 198 and notes—from which I learned of Enelow's work.

4. To be sure, there were classes and the privileges of class in ancient Israel: slave and free, poor and rich, commoner and noble, laity and priesthood. Moreover, even with God (as I said in the conclusion of lecture 1) the status of the pray-er counted, so that a prophet or righteous man might be especially effective as an intercessor. The point I wish to make here is that, in the matter of access to God, and the possibility of winning his favor (a fundamental measure of dignity), class and rank appear not to have been of themselves decisive either in theory or practice; and that extemporized prayer both derived from, and promoted, that tenet.

5. See Y. Kaufmann, *The Religion of Israel*, pp. 160-161, 366-367.

6. The crucial factors in this spiritual development—all worshipers having ready and constant access to the sole, high God, and his essential righteousness—were distinctively Israelite. "The normal custom of the Babylonians in time of need was to petition their personal gods. . . . For most Babylonians the personal deity was very minor, but it was his duty, if suitably provided with offerings by his client, to look after the latter as need arose" (W. Lambert, A. Millard, *Atrahasīs: The Babylonian Story of the Flood* [Oxford, 1969], p. 10). How he affected this by intercession with mightier, more influential gods is described by T. Jacobsen in H. and H. A. Frankfort

et al., *The Intellectual Adventure of Ancient Man* (Chicago, 1946), pp. 203-207. Nothing suggests that these minor deities were essentially moral or that their patronage was contingent on the morality of their clients. Even the high gods, who might serve as the personal gods of kings and great men, did not condition acceptance of prayer and worship on rectitude. "There was no distinction...between morally right and ritually proper. The god was just as angry with the eating of ritually impure food as with oppressing the widow and orphan. His anger would be appeased no less with the ritual offering than with a reformed life" (W. Lambert, "Morals in Ancient Mesopotamia," *Ex Oriente Lux* 15 (1957-1958), 194; this citation might well describe a vulgar Israelite's notion which the prophet railed against on the basis of Israel's singular God-concept). The obligations to personal gods, minor or major gods, were summed up thus by a Babylonian sage:

> Every day worship your god.
> Sacrifice and benediction are the proper accompaniment of
>   incense.
> Present your free-will offering to your god,
> For this is proper toward the gods.
> Prayer, supplication, and prostration
> Offer him daily and *you will get* your reward.
> Then you will have full communion with your god.
> In your wisdom study the tablet.
> Reverence begets favour,
> Sacrifice prolongs life,
> And prayer atones for guilt....
>   [W. G. Lambert, *Babylonian Wisdom Literature*
>   (Oxford, 1960), p. 105]

(Jacobsen's recent discussion in his *The Treasures of Darkness* [New Haven, 1976], pp. 147-164, stresses the paternal aspect of the personal god; this does not affect the point made here.)

The problematic relation of morality to religion in Egypt is notorious. "That Egyptian gods are in essence not ethical powers needs no emphasizing" (H. Bonnet, *Reallexikon der Aegyptischen Religionsgeschichte* [Berlin, 1971], p. 173). In the life of worship, including prayer, the utilitarian motive is dominant. The oft-quoted passage in the Instructions of Merikare, "The loaf of the upright is preferred to the ox of the evildoer" [M. Lichtheim, *Ancient Egyptian Literature*,

Vol I (Berkeley, Los Angeles, London, 1973), 106] is immediately followed by a pragmatic, ritual-centered view of worship:

> Work for the god, he will work for you also
> With offerings that make the altar flourish,
> With carvings that proclaim your name,
> God thinks of him who works for him.
>   [Lichtheim, ibid.]

The suffusion of worship by magic gravely impeded its ethical effect (see Bonnet, p. 175 f.).

Thus even if we allow the prevalence of a vital popular life of prayer among Israel's neighbors, the effect will not have been the same. The combination in Israel of the immediate accessibility of the high God to all Israelites, and his essential righteousness, was a crucial, fateful difference.

INDEX

Designer:	University of California Press Staff
Compositor:	Janet Sheila Brown
Printer:	Thomson-Shore, Inc.
Binder:	John H. Dekker & Sons
Text:	11/14 Paladium, Compuwriter II
Display:	Palatino